Thinking Critically

Thinking Critically: Gun Control and Violence

Andrea C. Nakaya

ReferencePoint Press®

San Diego, CA

About the Author

Andrea C. Nakaya, a native of New Zealand, holds a BA in English and an MA in Communications from San Diego State University. She currently lives in Encinitas, California, with her husband and their two children, Shane and Natalie.

© 2014 ReferencePoint Press, Inc.
Printed in the United States

For more information, contact:
ReferencePoint Press, Inc.
PO Box 27779
San Diego, CA 92198
www. ReferencePointPress.com

Cover credit: Thinkstock Images
Steve Zmina: 9, 16, 22, 29, 35, 42, 47, 56, 62

LIBRARY OF CONGRESS CATALOGING-IN-PUBLICATION DATA

Nakaya, Andrea C., 1976-
 Thinking critically : gun control and violence / by Andrea C. Nakaya.
  pages cm. -- (Thinking critically)
 title: Gun control and violence
 Includes bibliographical references and index.
 Audience: Grade 9 to 12.
 ISBN 978-1-60152-606-9 (hardback) -- ISBN 1-60152-606-7 (hardback) 1. Gun control--United States--Juvenile literature. 2. Violent crimes--United States--Juvenile literature. I. Title. II. Title: Gun control and violence.
  HV7436.N35 2014
  363.330973--dc23
                                                                    2013012392

Contents

Foreword

"Literacy is the most basic currency of the knowledge economy we're living in today." Barack Obama (at the time a senator from Illinois) spoke these words during a 2005 speech before the American Library Association. One question raised by this statement is: What does it mean to be a literate person in the twenty-first century?

E.D. Hirsch Jr., author of *Cultural Literacy: What Every American Needs to Know*, answers the question this way: "To be culturally literate is to possess the basic information needed to thrive in the modern world. The breadth of the information is great, extending over the major domains of human activity from sports to science."

But literacy in the twenty-first century goes beyond the accumulation of knowledge gained through study and experience and expanded over time. Now more than ever literacy requires the ability to sift through and evaluate vast amounts of information and, as the authors of the Common Core State Standards state, to "demonstrate the cogent reasoning and use of evidence that is essential to both private deliberation and responsible citizenship in a democratic republic."

The Thinking Critically series challenges students to become discerning readers, to think independently, and to engage and develop their skills as critical thinkers. Through a narrative-driven, pro/con format, the series introduces students to the complex issues that dominate public discourse—topics such as gun control and violence, social networking, and medical marijuana. All chapters revolve around a single, pointed question such as Can Stronger Gun Control Measures Prevent Mass Shootings?, or Does Social Networking Benefit Society?, or Should Medical Marijuana Be Legalized? This inquiry-based approach introduces student researchers to core issues and concerns on a given topic. Each chapter includes one part that argues the affirmative and one part that argues the negative—all written by a single author. With the single-author format the predominant arguments for and against an issue can be synthesized into clear, accessible discussions supported by details and evidence including relevant facts, direct quotes, current examples, and statistical illustrations. All volumes include focus questions to guide students as they read each pro/con discussion, a list of key facts, and an annotated list of related organizations and websites for conducting further research.

The authors of the Common Core State Standards have set out the particular qualities that a literate person in the twenty-first century must have. These include the ability to think independently, establish a base of knowledge across a wide range of subjects, engage in open-minded but discerning reading and listening, know how to use and evaluate evidence, and appreciate and understand diverse perspectives. The new Thinking Critically series supports these goals by providing a solid introduction to the study of pro/con issues.

Gun Control and Violence

On the morning of December 14, 2012, twenty-year-old Adam Lanza used his mother's rifle to shoot her four times in the head, killing her while she slept in their Newtown, Connecticut, home. He then drove to Sandy Hook Elementary School with the rifle and other guns from his mother's collection. After shooting the principal and school psychologist, he walked into a first-grade classroom, where he shot and killed the teacher and fifteen of the sixteen students. Only one person in the room survived, a six-year-old girl who played dead until Lanza was gone. Lanza continued his killing spree throughout the school, killing a total of twenty children and six adults, wounding two others, and then finally shooting himself.

People across the nation were shocked and saddened to hear about the Newtown tragedy. Even President Barack Obama was in tears as he addressed the press. Yet mass shootings are not uncommon in the United States. Just four months earlier, a gunman killed six people and wounded four others at a Sikh temple in Wisconsin, and only a month before that another gunman at an Aurora, Colorado, movie theater killed twelve people and injured fifty-eight.

The United States has the highest gun ownership rate in the world. It also has a very high rate of gun-related death and injury. Statistics such as these call into question whether Americans need more gun restrictions and whether such restrictions should govern who can purchase and carry guns. Whether controlling guns would prevent mass shootings such as the one in Newtown remains a matter of debate.

More Guns than Any Other Country

It is widely agreed that compared with other countries, the United States has a very large number of guns. According to the most recent statistics, it has the most firearms per person of any country in the world. Yemen is ranked second and Switzerland third, yet they are far behind the United States. The Small Arms Survey, which conducts extensive research on firearms around the world, estimates that the United States has about eighty-nine guns for every one hundred people, while Yemen has only about fifty-five. In a 2012 investigative report published in *Mother Jones* magazine, the authors found that in recent years, the number of firearms in the United States has increased more quickly than the population. The report found that between 1995 and 2012, the number of guns increased by about 50 percent, while the population increased by only 20 percent.

Yet although the United States has an extremely high rate of ownership and an increasing number of guns, the majority of Americans do not own guns. This is because the people who do own them often have more than one. The General Social Survey, which has been conducted in the United States since 1972, reports that about a third of Americans own guns.

High Rate of Gun-Related Crime

In addition to possessing a large number of guns compared with other countries, the United States also experiences a high occurrence of gun-related crime and injury. For example, it has the highest rate of gun-related homicide for any developed nation. According to the most recent data reported by the United Nations Office on Drugs and Crime, in 2010 the percentage of homicides committed with firearms was 67.5 in the United States. In 2009 (the most recent statistics available), Canada's was 32 percent, and in the United Kingdom it was 6.6 percent. The Brady Campaign to Prevent Gun Violence, a gun control advocacy group, estimates that each year 97,820 people are shot in America, or an average of 268 per day.

One form of gun-related violence that happens more often in the United States than in any other developed country is mass shootings. *Mother Jones* reports that since 1982 at least sixty-two mass murders committed in the United States involved firearms. The shootings occurred in thirty different states.

The Second Amendment and Gun Laws

The Second Amendment to the Constitution is an important part of the gun control debate in the United States because it specifically mentions the right to bear arms. However, due to its unclear wording, a heated dispute occurs over exactly how far that right should extend. The amendment says, "A well regulated militia being necessary to the security of a free state, the right of the people to keep and bear arms shall not be infringed." Americans disagree over the interpretation of this sentence and whether the right to bear arms applies to the militia or to private citizens.

Before 2008 Americans generally believed that the right to bear arms was a collective right—for example, the right to bear arms was meant to describe taking part in the military. However, two Supreme Court decisions changed this interpretation. In 2008 and 2010 the court ruled that the Second Amendment does give individuals the right to possess and carry firearms. However, these decisions did not eliminate the ongoing debate. As author and political columnist Joe Klein points out, even if the right to bear arms is guaranteed by the Constitution, it still has to be subject to some kind of regulation. He explains, "No right is absolute. No American has the right to own a stealth bomber or a nuclear weapon. Armor-piercing bullets are forbidden. The question is where you draw a reasonable line."[1] The question of where to draw the line on gun regulation continues to be the topic of intense disagreement.

> "No right is absolute. No American has the right to own a stealth bomber or a nuclear weapon. Armor-piercing bullets are forbidden. The question is where you draw a reasonable line."[1]
>
> —Joe Klein is an author and political columnist.

Firearms and Homicides: A Global View

The United States has more firearms per capita than any country in the world and the highest rate of firearm-related homicides among the world's most developed nations, according to a 2012 report by the Council on Foreign Relations. Some analysts say such statistics show a clear cause-and-effect relationship while others argue that many factors, not just the number of guns, help explain the high rate of firearm-related homicides in the United States.

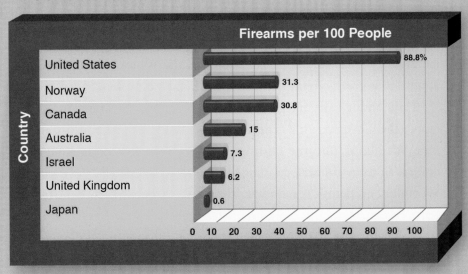

Firearms per 100 People

Country	Value
United States	88.8%
Norway	31.3
Canada	30.8
Australia	15
Israel	7.3
United Kingdom	6.2
Japan	0.6

Firearm Homicides per 100,000

Country	Value
United States	3.21
Canada	0.51
Australia	0.14
Israel	0.09
United Kingdom	0.07
Norway	0.05
Japan	0.01

Source: Jonathan Masters, "U.S. Gun Policy: Global Comparisons," Council on Foreign Relations, December 21, 2012. www.cfr.org.

Gun Laws in the United States

Current gun laws in the United States vary by state. However, all businesses that sell firearms must be federally licensed. Federal law also requires that these businesses conduct background checks on the people they sell guns to. Certain groups of people are not allowed to purchase firearms, including those who have ever been committed to a mental institution and people with a criminal record. Despite the law, though, some people avoid background checks by purchasing a gun from a private seller where a check is not required—for example, at a gun show. Research shows that large numbers of people purchase guns this way. In its 2013 report on reducing gun violence, the White House stated that almost 40 percent of gun sales are made by private sellers.

Laws about carrying guns in public also vary by state. In a 2012 report the Government Accountability Office (GAO) found that every state but Illinois and the District of Columbia issues permits allowing citizens to carry concealed handguns. In Vermont, Alaska, Arizona, and Wyoming, no permit is required. The GAO also reports that thirty-nine states recognize permits from other states.

Following the 2012 Newtown shooting, Obama urged Congress to pass laws that would help reduce gun violence. Among the steps he and Vice President Joseph Biden have proposed are background checks for all gun sales and a ban on assault weapons and high-capacity magazines. Numerous states, including New York and California, have also made efforts to more strictly regulate firearms. However, overall, most experts agree that gun control laws have actually become less strict in recent years. Journalist Mark Follman cautions that a lenient law in one state can significantly impact other states. This is because many states recognize laws from other states—for example, handgun permits. He warns, "We're on our way to a situation where the most lax state permitting rules—say, Virginia's, where an online course now qualifies for firearms safety training and has drawn a flood of out-of-state applicants—are in effect national law."[2]

Some types of guns and ammunition are not legal for the general population in the United States. For example, the National Firearms Act of 1934 prohibits civilians from owning fully automatic weapons (which fire continuously when the trigger is held down) and short-barreled shotguns. Critics argue a ban should extend to semiautomatic rifles that can rapidly fire multiple rounds, as well as to magazines that hold many bullets. In 1994 the United States did impose such a ban, making it illegal to manufacture or purchase certain types of semiautomatic weapons and high-capacity magazines. The types of guns prohibited under the Federal Assault Weapons Ban are commonly called "assault weapons." (A true assault rifle is a type of gun used by the military and is illegal for civilian use.) However, the ban was widely critiqued as ineffective because it had too many exceptions. It expired in 2004.

> "There already exists nearly enough guns in this country to arm every man, woman, and child in America. And many of these tools are simple and sturdy enough to remain accurate and functional for generations."[3]
>
> —Christopher Matthews is a reporter for *Time* magazine.

A Controversial Issue

Gun control is an extremely controversial issue in the United States, with fervent supporters of both sides. Americans continually debate gun control laws and whether they should be changed. Each time a mass shooting occurs, that discussion gets even more heated. Regardless of the direction the debate takes, though, the fact is that the United States has a huge number of guns and is likely to have them for a long time. Says *Time* reporter Christopher Matthews, "There already exists nearly enough guns in this country to arm every man, woman, and child in America. And many of these tools are simple and sturdy enough to remain accurate and functional for generations."[3] No matter which side of the issue one takes on gun control, then, the likelihood that it will remain an issue is guaranteed.

Chapter One

Do Americans Have a Constitutional Right to Own Guns?

Americans Have a Constitutional Right to Own Guns

- The Second Amendment guarantees the individual right to own a gun.
- The constitutional right to own a gun is important because it gives individuals the ability to protect themselves.
- Owning a gun is an important part of America's culture.
- The US Supreme Court has affirmed that the Constitution protects the individual right to own a gun.

The Debate at a Glance

Americans Do Not Have a Constitutional Right to Own Guns

- The Second Amendment guarantees the right to bear arms as part of a militia.
- The belief that Americans have an individual right to own a gun has been advanced by political groups and is not supported by the Constitution.
- Individual gun ownership is not an effective way to protect America's democracy.
- The right to own a gun must be restricted in order to protect the freedom of others.

Americans Have a Constitutional Right to Own Guns

"I, like most Americans, believe that the Second Amendment guarantees an individual the right to bear arms."

Barack Obama, speech at the National Urban League Convention, New Orleans, July 25, 2012.

Consider these questions as you read:

1. Do you agree that if the right to own a gun is taken away from Americans, then other constitutional rights will also be at risk? Why or why not?
2. How persuasive is the argument that people need to own guns in order to protect themselves from government oppression? Which arguments provide the strongest support for this perspective, and why?
3. Can you think of an example where the right of one citizen to own a gun might conflict with the rights of other citizens? Explain.

Editor's note: The discussion that follows presents common arguments made in support of this perspective, reinforced by facts, quotes, and examples taken from various sources.

The right to own a gun is guaranteed by the US Constitution, and the government should ensure this right. When the country was founded, its citizens recognized that they had certain basic rights such as the freedom of speech and of self-defense. The right to bear arms is one of these basic rights. The Second Amendment says, "The right of the people to keep and bear arms shall not be infringed," meaning that Americans have a right to own and carry guns if they so choose. The Second Amendment Foundation, an organization that works to protect gun rights, insists that all constitutional rights must be protected, even if they are unpopular with some people, or the freedom of all Americans will be threatened.

The foundation says, "In our constitution, gun ownership is protected just like freedom of speech, and the freedom from cruel and unusual punishment. We believe that the Bill of Rights are interdependent, in other words that you cannot pick which ones to honor, and which ones to ignore. If this is allowed, no civil rights are safe."[4]

Self-Defense

One reason the Constitution guarantees the right to own a gun is so that people have the ability to protect themselves from harm. While law enforcement exists to protect citizens from criminals, it is impossible for police to be present to prevent every crime. In some cases individuals do not have time to wait for the police to arrive, so they must defend themselves. A gun is an effective way to do so. Denny Peyman, a sheriff in eastern Kentucky, insists that people are safer if they have a gun. He says, "There are some places in this county that [it] takes me 45 minutes to get to. If they have a gun, they could do a better job of defending themselves than waiting for me."[5] Even in places where law enforcement is able to arrive more quickly, it may not arrive soon enough, and citizens should have the ability to protect themselves if they so choose.

> "In our constitution, gun ownership is protected just like freedom of speech, and the freedom from cruel and unusual punishment."[4]
>
> —The Second Amendment Foundation, an organization that promotes the constitutional right to privately own firearms.

Stories abound about people who might have been killed or injured by criminals if they had not had a gun to protect themselves. For example, on New Year's Eve 2011, Sarah McKinley, an eighteen-year-old Oklahoma mother, was alone in her house with her three-month-old baby when two men tried to break in. McKinley barricaded the door with a couch and called 911, but law enforcement officers did not arrive in time to help her. One of the intruders broke open the door and entered the house with a 12-inch (30.5 cm) hunting knife in his hand. McKinley says that she saw something shimmering in his hand and thought it was a pistol. Believing that the man intended to harm her, she used her gun to shoot him and protect herself and her baby. McKinley says she does not regret shooting the intruder. She says, "We could have been in a whole different situation if I hadn't done it."[6]

Protection from Government

The constitutional right to own a gun also helps individuals protect themselves from the government. History reveals that governments sometimes use their power to harm and oppress citizens. The people who wrote the Second Amendment wanted to ensure that Americans could protect themselves from any such abuse of power. They understood that if weapons were exclusively under the control of the government, then liberty was threatened. Journalist Jack Kenny says, "For liberty to be secure, it was necessary that weapons be in the hands of the people and not entrusted only to a professional standing army." He explains that while in many cases a standing army helps protect citizens, it is also a potential danger. He says, "While armies might be needed to repel external threats, they were also seen as temptations to tyrants who would use them to subdue and oppress the people."[7]

Kenny points out that at many times in history, citizens who have been disarmed by their government have been defenseless in cases when the government later used standing armies to oppress them. Adolf Hitler, Josef Stalin, and Mao Tse-tung—famous leaders who killed thousands of innocent people in the countries they ruled—all faced less opposition because the population had been largely disarmed and was unable to fight back. For example, Stalin was the leader of the Soviet Union from the mid-1920s until 1953, and under his rule access to guns was restricted. Stalin executed hundreds of thousands of people who were opposed to his leadership, and he imprisoned millions in labor camps.

Kenny agrees that allowing private citizens to be armed can be risky. For example, it is easier for a disturbed individual to obtain a gun and carry out a mass shooting. However, he believes it is more risky to give

Majority of Americans Believe They Have a Right to Own a Gun

The US Supreme Court has ruled that Americans have a constitutional right to own a gun, and public opinion polls show that the majority of Americans agree with this view. This graph shows the results of Gallup polls between 1959 and 2013 regarding the right to own a handgun, the most popular type of gun owned by Americans. It reveals that 74 percent of Americans are opposed to a ban on these guns, a record high since Gallup began asking this question. Twenty-four percent are in favor of a ban.

Do you think there should or should not be a law that would ban the possession of handguns, except by the police and other authorized persons?

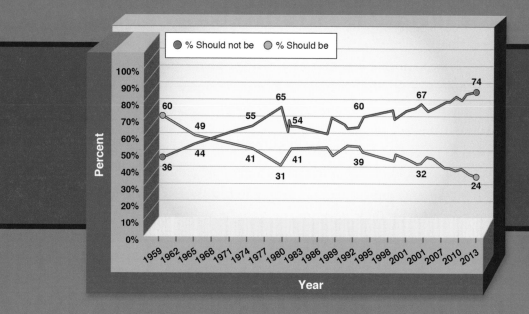

Source: Gallup, "Americans Want Stricter Gun Laws, Still Oppose Bans," December 27, 2012. www.gallup.com.

the government a monopoly on guns. He says, "A depraved killer or two . . . may kill a dozen or more people at a school, shopping mall, or movie theater before being killed or captured. Governments with legal monopolies on lethal weapons have in the past century killed people by the millions."[8]

Hunting

In addition to facilitating self-defense, guns are an important part of America's national heritage. Large numbers of Americans collect them or use them for hunting or target practice. In many families guns are treasured family heirlooms that are passed down through generations. Barack Obama affirmed the cultural importance of gun ownership in the United States in a 2012 speech addressing gun laws. He said, "We recognize the traditions of gun ownership that passed on from genera-

tion to generation—that hunting and shooting are part of a cherished national heritage."[9] Senator Mark Udall talks about how guns are an integral part of life in Colorado, where he grew up, and says that gun culture has played a role in shaping who he is today. He says, "Having grown up in the West, I have a deep appreciation for our outdoor heritage. As a kid I learned how to shoot a rifle, and as an instructor and later executive director of Colorado Outward Bound, I

> "We recognize the traditions of gun ownership that passed on from generation to generation—that hunting and shooting are part of a cherished national heritage."[9]
>
> —Barack Obama, the forty-fourth president of the United States.

developed a great respect for Colorado's wildlife and habitat." According to Udall, "Gun-ownership, hunting and fishing are all a part of the way of life in the West."[10] Taking away the right to own a gun would be taking away an important part of American culture.

Supreme Court Rulings

The US Supreme Court has affirmed that the Second Amendment guarantees the individual right to own and carry guns. Two decisions officially establish this. In 2008's *District of Columbia v. Heller*, the court ruled in the case of a Washington, DC, security guard. At that time, the guard was not allowed to keep his handgun at home because of strict rules in the District of Columbia that essentially banned handguns. The court found that these regulations were unconstitutional because they violated the Second Amendment. According to the court, "There seems to us to be no doubt, on the basis of both text and history, that the Second Amendment conferred an individual right to keep and bear arms."[11] In its decision the court makes the interpretation that under the Second Amendment, an individual has the right to use a gun for traditionally lawful purposes such as self-defense in the home and that this right is unconnected to service in a militia.

In 2010 the court again recognized that individuals have a constitutional right to own guns. In *McDonald v. Chicago*, a Chicago resident wanted to purchase a handgun for personal home defense, yet was prevented from doing so by a city law. The court ruled that the law was unconstitutional because like the federal government, state and local governments cannot pass laws that infringe on the individual's right to bear arms for self-defense in the home. As in its 2008 decision, the court affirmed that the Second Amendment guarantees the individual right to own a gun, stating, "It is clear that the Framers . . . counted the right to keep and bear arms among those fundamental rights necessary to our system of ordered liberty."[12]

Since the founding of the United States, American citizens have taken pride in their liberty and rejected any attempt to take it away. The right of an individual to own a gun is part of that liberty. It is guaranteed by the Constitution and should not be restricted.

Americans Do Not Have a Constitutional Right to Own Guns

"The Second Amendment protects a collective right rather than an individual right [to own guns]."

ACLU, "Second Amendment," January 17, 2013. www.aclu.org.

Consider these questions as you read:

1. Do you agree with the argument that the text of the Second Amendment is ambiguous and difficult to interpret? Why or why not?
2. Societal interpretations of the Second Amendment have changed over time in the United States. Why do you think this has happened?
3. How persuasive is the argument that individual gun ownership is not the best way to protect democracy? Can you think of a case when individual citizens might need guns in order to protect themselves from the government?

Editor's note: The discussion that follows presents common arguments made in support of this perspective, reinforced by facts, quotes, and examples taken from various sources.

The US Constitution does not state that individuals have the right to own guns. The text of the Second Amendment reads: "A well regulated militia, being necessary to the security of a free state, the right of the people to keep and bear arms shall not be infringed." While this sentence clearly mentions the right to keep and bear arms, it is ungrammatical and difficult to interpret. As a result, based simply on a reading of the Second Amendment, it is impossible to definitively say that it guarantees the individual right to bear arms. Because of its difficult wording, the amendment has been interpreted a number of different ways, and overall, the public disagrees about what it means. National Public Radio correspondent Linton Weeks says, "After more than 200 years of intense scrutiny by people more versed in The Law than you and I . . . the meaning of the Second Amendment continues to baffle and elude."[13]

The Original Intent

As a result of such ambiguity, interpretation of the Second Amendment should be based on how it was understood at the time it was written. An examination of the history and context of the amendment reveals that it was actually intended to guarantee the right to an armed militia, not the individual right to bear arms. When the Constitution and the Bill of Rights were created, the United States was trying to establish a strong central government. A militia was needed to support that government. As sociologist Keith Darling-Brekhus explains, "The Constitution was drawn up to expand, not shrink the power of the national government." He argues, "The Second Amendment portion was added to provide for domestic order and peace and the Second Amendment called for a 'well-regulated militia' to provide for the 'security of a free state.'"[14]

At the time the Second Amendment was written, this interpretation was taken for granted by the population. However, states no longer have militias like they did when the Constitution was written, so Americans now misinterpret the Second Amendment, arguing that it allows for the individual right to bear arms. Legal analyst Jeffrey Toobin says, "What makes this subject so difficult in the modern world is that state militias don't exist anymore, so we have no familiarity with what a state militia is." But according to Toobin, "It was simply taken as a given in constitutional law that the Second Amendment did not give individuals a right to bear arms."[15]

> "It was simply taken as a given in constitutional law that the Second Amendment did not give individuals a right to bear arms."[15]
>
> —Jeffrey Toobin is a lawyer and journalist.

A Recent Interpretation

The belief that the Constitution guarantees individuals the right to bear arms is a recent interpretation. For most of US history, courts actually rejected the argument that the Second Amendment protects the individual right to bear arms. It was not until 2008 that the Supreme Court held that the Second Amendment protects an individual right to have guns. In *District of Columbia v. Heller*, the court ruled that an individual has the right to possess a gun for personal use such as self-defense. Prior to 2008, however, the leading decision of the court was *United States v. Miller*. That ruling stated that the Second Amendment guarantee is connected to the preservation of a militia.

Political Interests

The recent interpretation that the Second Amendment protects individual gun rights is significantly impacted by political interests rather than the actual text of the amendment. Court decisions about the meaning of the amendment—such as the landmark *District of Columbia v. Heller* decision in 2008—depend on the beliefs of the particular judges in power, and which judges make those decisions depends on who appoints them to their position. So how the Second Amendment is interpreted is largely dependent on politics. Toobin says, "What the Second Amendment means is not determined by the Second Amendment, it's determined by who wins presidential elections and gets to appoint their like-minded justices. These decisions about what the Constitution means are deeply political. Always have been, always will be."[16]

The National Rifle Association (NRA), a large and powerful organization that promotes the right of citizens to bear arms, has also had a significant impact on the interpretation of the Second Amendment. In addition to promoting firearms safety, the NRA strongly supports the right of law-abiding Americans to own and use firearms and insists that this right is constitutionally guaranteed. The NRA is one of the most powerful lobbying organizations in Congress and has used its power to influence the way the courts and the government view the Second Amendment. In a 2013 speech, Wayne LaPierre, CEO of the NRA, states that the organization has 4.5 million active members and tens of millions of supporters. The *Huffington Post* reports that in 2012 the organization spent $3 million on lobbying the federal government and millions more on other political contributions. Lobbying and other political contribu-

Gun Rights Are Not Absolute

While many Americans believe that citizens have the right to own guns, they also believe that this constitutional right is not absolute and must be balanced against other rights. These graphs show the results of a December 2012 poll of eighteen hundred people. The first reveals that the majority believe that protecting people from violent gun-related crimes is more important than protecting the rights of gun owners. According to the second graph, only a small percentage of people feel that stronger gun violence prevention legislation would infringe on Second Amendment rights.

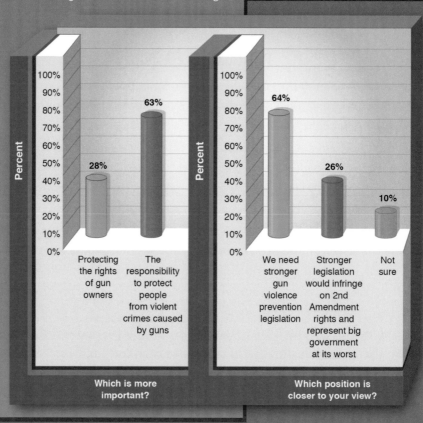

Source: Douglas E. Schoen, "National Gun Survey—Interested Parties Memo," January 2013. http://libcloud.s3.amazonaws.com.

tions are made in order to influence legislation, including gun control legislation.

Debra Maggart, a former member of the Tennessee House of Representatives, says that she knows from experience how powerful the NRA is. According to Maggart, because of the fact that she disagreed with the NRA on a bill related to gun rights, the organization spent $155,000 to defeat her in 2012 elections for the state legislature. She says the NRA's campaign against her included radio and newspaper ads, a Defeat Maggart website, a YouTube video, and multiple mailings. Maggart believes the NRA has a lot of power over legislators. She says, "Because of N.R.A. bully tactics, legislators are not free to openly discuss the merits of gun-related legislation. This stifling of discussion does not serve the interest of the public nor of the gun owners. But the N.R.A. gets their way because they know how intimidating they are and they know that lawmakers are afraid to speak openly about what needs to be done."[17]

Not the Best Way to Protect Democracy

Another argument gun rights advocates make is that the individual right to own a gun is an important safeguard of democracy. They argue that if the government has a monopoly on arms, it might use that power for harm and that the individual right to bear arms is essential because it gives citizens the power to protect their democracy. History does show that governments sometimes abuse their power and use it to oppress the people they govern. But allowing individuals to own guns will do nothing to prevent such abuse. In its blog, *Democracy in America*, the *Economist* insists that such a position is ridiculous. It points out that governments and weapons have become so powerful that it would take a lot more than guns to protect a population from government oppression. If the United States really wants to give its population the ability to protect itself from government oppression, the *Economist* says,

> then the entire regime of current gun restrictions needs to be overturned: citizens need to be able to buy fully automatic assault rifles, rocket launchers, military-grade explosives, remote detonators, armoured vehicles with mounted artillery, surface-to-air missiles, light bombers, armed drones, everything. If some citizens want to keep and bear arms in order to take on the power of the federal government, that's what it's going to take.[18]

Balancing Rights

While individual rights and freedoms are important in the United States and are protected by the Constitution, these rights are not absolute, because they must be balanced with the rights of society. Like all rights, gun ownership must be subject to some restriction for the benefit of society. Harvard College administrator Erika Christakis points out that no constitutional rights are absolute. She says, "Constitutionally protected freedoms are routinely curtailed in the name of public safety, morality, or even convenience." According to Christakis, "Our right to free speech is routinely regulated through obscenity laws. Slander, libel, pornography; we're muzzled all the time. So, too, are our rights to assembly and religion compromised. You can't stage a protest at noon in the middle of Times Square. A parent can't deny a child lifesaving medical care or education."[19] Even the Supreme Court recognizes that restrictions on constitutional freedoms are necessary. In a 2008 decision about firearms in *District of Columbia v. Heller*, Justice Antonin Scalia stated, "Like most rights, the Second Amendment right is not unlimited."[20]

Individual gun rights are not constitutionally guaranteed in the United States. The belief that they are is a result of misinterpretation of the Second Amendment, and the powerful influence of various political groups.

> "Constitutionally protected freedoms are routinely curtailed in the name of public safety, morality, or even convenience."[19]
>
> —Erika Christakis is an administrator at Harvard College.

Chapter Two

Are More Restrictions on Who Can Purchase and Carry Guns Needed?

More Restrictions on Who Can Purchase and Carry Guns Are Needed

- The United States should enforce universal background checks and stricter concealed-carry laws.
- Gun control laws should be the same in every state.
- The widespread availability of guns makes society more dangerous for everyone, so guns should be restricted.
- Statistics show that strict gun control laws reduce crime.

The Debate at a Glance

More Restrictions on Who Can Purchase and Carry Guns Are Unnecessary

- Guns allow people to protect themselves and deter crime, so they should not be restricted.
- The government should enforce existing laws, not create new ones.
- Universal background checks will not stop criminals from obtaining guns and are a threat to civil rights.
- There is no evidence that strict gun control laws reduce crime.

More Restrictions on Who Can Purchase and Carry Guns Are Needed

"Poorly regulated firearms have become a major THREAT in everyday American life. . . . Strong, sensible gun safety legislation is way overdue."

Ken Swain, statement at Mental Health Services Working Group Public Hearing Testimony, Connecticut General Assembly, January 29, 2013. www.cga.ct.gov.

Consider these questions as you read:

1. The city of New York undercover gun show investigation reveals that it can be very easy to obtain a gun without any kind of screening. Do you think the United States needs to pass laws to change this? Why or why not?
2. Do you agree with the argument that the federal government should pass strong federal laws and enforce the same laws in every state, or do you think that each state should be allowed to regulate guns? Explain your answer.
3. How strong is the argument that strict gun control reduces crime? Which argument do you think is the more persuasive? Why?

Editor's note: The discussion that follows presents common arguments made in support of this perspective, reinforced by facts, quotes, and examples taken from various sources.

The United States has some of the least restrictive gun laws of any developed nation, making it relatively easy for an individual to purchase and carry a gun. One of the easiest places to purchase a gun is at a gun show, where sellers are not required to run background checks to screen potential purchasers for things such as mental illness or a criminal record. In 2011 investigators in Gun Show Undercover: Arizona—a project undertaken by the city of New York—went to an

Arizona gun show in an attempt to find out just how easy it was to buy a gun. Undercover investigators easily purchased multiple guns by simply showing a driver's license. One investigator was able to buy two 9-millimeter pistols from different sellers even after he told them both, "I probably couldn't pass a background check."[21] Selling to someone who cannot pass a background check is a federal felony. Overall, the city of New York reports that it investigated seven gun shows in three states and that thirty-five of the forty-seven sellers who were approached sold guns illegally.

Require Background Checks

As this investigation reveals, it is easy for anyone—even a criminal or someone with criminal intent—to buy a gun in the United States. In order to prevent potentially dangerous individuals from obtaining fire-arms, the government should ensure that every individual purchasing a gun is subject to a federal background check. While federal law does actually require background checks for gun purchases, private sellers—such as those at gun shows—are exempt. The White House estimates that almost 40 percent of gun sales are made by private sellers. This means that a large number of people are buying guns without under-going a background check. Barack Obama believes this should change. He says:

> I believe the majority of gun owners would agree that we should do everything possible to prevent criminals and fugitives from purchasing weapons; that we should check someone's criminal record before they can check out a gun seller; that a mentally unbalanced individual should not be able to get his hands on a gun so easily. These steps shouldn't be controversial. They should be common sense.[22]

A December 2012 Gallup poll shows that most Americans agree; 92 percent of those surveyed are in favor of laws that require background checks for people attempting to purchase guns.

Stricter Concealed-Carry Laws

The United States should also have tougher restrictions on carrying concealed weapons in public places. While some states do have tough restrictions and grant permits only at the discretion of law enforcement authorities, the majority of US states are classified as "shall issue" states. This means that individuals are guaranteed a permit as long as they meet certain requirements set by the state—for example, background checks, age requirements, and firearms safety classes. When permits are easy to obtain and a large number of people walk around in public with guns, the risk is high that some of these guns will be used for harm—for example, by accident or in a moment of stress or anger. John Gilchrist, legislative counsel for the Ohio Association of Chiefs of Police, argues, "There wouldn't be as much gun violence if we didn't have people carrying weapons. If you've got people walking around in a bad mood—or in a divorce, they've lost their job—and they get into a confrontation, this could result in the use of a gun."[23]

> "There wouldn't be as much gun violence if we didn't have people carrying weapons."[23]
>
> —John Gilchrist, legislative counsel for the Ohio Association of Chiefs of Police.

Universal Enforcement

In addition to placing more restrictions on the purchase and carrying of guns, the United States needs to ensure that every state enforces these restrictions, or they will be ineffective. At present, the United States has many different gun laws, and while some are strict, many are not. The weak laws take away the power of the strong ones. For example, someone who wants to obtain a weapon or ammunition can simply obtain it in one of those states that does not have strict gun control laws. Gene Voegtlin of the International Association of Chiefs of Police says, "The patchwork of laws in many ways means that the laws are only as effective as the weakest law there is. Those that are trying to acquire firearms and may not be able to do that by walking into their local gun shop will try to find a way to do that. This patchwork of laws allows them to seek out the weak links and acquire weapons."[24]

Stronger Gun Laws Are Associated with Fewer Gun Deaths

Strict limits on the purchase and carrying of guns are associated with fewer gun-related deaths. As can be seen in this chart, seven of the ten states with the strongest gun laws also have the lowest gun death rates, indicating a correlation between strong laws and low death rates.

Top 10 States with the Strongest Gun Laws		Top 10 States with the Lowest Gun Death Rates
1. California		1. Hawaii
2. New Jersey		2. Massachusetts
3. Massachusetts	7 States Have Both	3. Rhode Island
4. Connecticut		4. New York
5. Hawaii		5. New Jersey
6. New York		6. Connecticut
7. Maryland		7. Minnesota
8. Illinois		8. Iowa
9. Rhode Island		9. California
10. Michigan		10. Maine

Source: Law Center to Prevent Gun Violence, "Gun Laws Matter 2012: Understanding the Link Between Weak Laws and Gun Violence," November 14, 2012. http://smartgunlaws.org.

More Dangerous for Everyone

Gun advocates argue that when people have guns they are safer because they have the ability to protect themselves. However, the reality is that when more people obtain guns to protect themselves, society actually becomes less safe overall. Philosophy professor and gun control expert Jeff McMahan describes how this happens. He says that when people obtain guns for protection, criminals respond by obtaining better guns to gain the upper hand. This encourages police to get even better weapons in an attempt to remain in power. As a result, the unarmed are more likely to feel vulnerable and obtain guns to protect themselves. McMahan says,

"The logic is inexorable: as more private individuals acquire guns, the power of the police declines, personal security becomes more a matter of self-help, and the unarmed have an increasing incentive to get guns, until everyone is armed." Overall, he says, society is less safe: "When most citizens then have the ability to kill anyone in their vicinity in an instant, everyone is less secure than they would be if no one had guns other than the members of a democratically accountable police force."[25]

> "When most citizens then have the ability to kill anyone in their vicinity in an instant, everyone is less secure than they would be if no one had guns other than the members of a democratically accountable police force."[25]
>
> —Jeff McMahan, a philosophy professor and gun control expert.

Statistics show that having a gun can actually increase the chance of a person being injured. For example, in 2009 researchers reported in the *American Journal of Public Health* about their study of people living in Philadelphia. They found that those people who owned a gun were 4.46 times more likely to be shot in an assault than those people who did not own a gun. Says journalist Larry Womack, "It turns out that guns, outside the hands of the military or law enforcement, just aren't any good at preventing crime and, in fact, their presence is associated with an increase in the likelihood of tragedy."[26]

Strict Gun Control Means Less Crime

Statistics actually show a correlation between strict gun control laws and lower rates of violent crime. The United States, with some of the least-strict gun laws in the world, has one of the highest rates of gun-related homicide among developed nations. In comparison, a number of countries with strict gun control laws have low rates. For example, Japan has very few guns due to some of the strictest laws in the world, and almost no gun-related homicides. In 2008, whereas more than twelve thousand gun-related homicides occurred in the United States, only eleven occurred in Japan. Gun-related crime has been greatly reduced in Great

Britain due to stronger gun control laws. According to the *Economist*, significantly fewer guns and bullets has also meant significantly less gun-related crime there. For example, it argues that the number of crimes involving guns dropped by 16 percent in 2011, and gunshot wounds have declined from 1,370 in 2003 to 972 in 2011.

Journalist Fareed Zakaria discounts arguments that factors other than gun laws cause the high rate of gun-related death and injury in the United States. He says, "Many people believe that America is simply a more violent, individualistic society. But again, the data clarify. For most crimes—theft, burglary, robbery, assault—the United States is within the range of other advanced countries. The category in which the U.S. rate is magnitudes higher is gun homicides." Zakaria insists that the reason for the high rate of shootings is the high rate of gun ownership, far higher than most other countries in the world. He says, "The data in social science are rarely this clear. They strongly suggest that we have so much more gun violence than other countries because we have far more permissive laws than others regarding the sale and possession of guns."[27]

To reduce the myriad negative effects it experiences due to the easy availability of guns, the United States should place more restrictions on who can purchase and carry firearms. In addition, it should make sure these restrictions are enforced in all situations and in all parts of the country.

More Restrictions on Who Can Purchase and Carry Guns Are Unnecessary

"[New restrictions] won't make anyone safer but . . . will interfere with a citizen's ability to acquire, keep and rely on firearms to protect their families or participate in the shooting sports."

David Keene, "NRA Chief: Why We Fight for Gun Rights," CNN, February 1, 2012. www.cnn.com.

Consider these questions as you read:

1. Do you agree with the argument that the best way to deter crime is to carry a gun? Why or why not?
2. Critics of universal background checks argue that these checks would violate some people's civil rights. Do you think that a reduction in civil rights might ever be necessary for the greater good of society? Why or why not?
3. Taking into account the facts and ideas presented in this discussion, how persuasive is the argument that the United States should not create new gun restrictions? Which facts and ideas are strongest, and why?

Editor's note: The discussion that follows presents common arguments made in support of this perspective, reinforced by facts, quotes, and examples taken from various sources.

In January 2013 a woman was at home with her nine-year-old twins in Loganville, Georgia, when an intruder forced himself into the house. She and her children hid, but as the man walked through the house, he found them. Using her .38 revolver, the woman fired six bullets at him, severely injuring him. This allowed the woman and her children to run from the house and call the police. As this story shows, guns are an effective tool for self-defense. People in the United States should be allowed to purchase and carry guns in order to defend themselves in situations such as this. They should not face more restrictions preventing them from doing so. While the Loganville criminal did not carry a weapon, many criminals are armed, making it even more essential to possess a gun for self-defense. Wayne LaPierre, CEO of the NRA, insists, "The *only* thing that stops a *bad* guy with a gun is a *good* guy with a gun." He argues that to effectively protect themselves in an emergency, people need access to their own gun. He asks, "Would you rather have your 911 call bring a good guy with a gun from a *mile* away . . . or a *minute* away?"[28]

> "The *only* thing that stops a *bad* guy with a gun is a *good* guy with a gun."[28]
>
> —Wayne LaPierre, CEO of the NRA.

Guns Deter Crime

Allowing people to own and carry guns actually deters crime, because if a criminal knows that his or her potential victim is armed and able to fight back, the criminal is less likely to approach the person. Explains gun-rights advocate John Lott, "You deter criminality by making it riskier for people to commit crimes. And one way to make it riskier is to create the impression among the criminal population that the law-abiding citizen they want to target may have a gun."[29]

Lott uses the 2012 Aurora movie theater shooting to illustrate his point. In that incident a gunman entered a Colorado movie theater during a midnight screening of the film *The Dark Knight Rises*. After setting off tear gas grenades, he shot into the audience with multiple guns, killing twelve people and injuring fifty-eight. The youngest victim was a six-year-old girl. Lott points out that this shooting happened at a theater that banned guns. He argues that the shooter intentionally picked the theater for that reason, knowing that the theatergoers would all be without guns and thus defenseless. Lott says:

> There were seven movie theaters showing the premiere of the Batman movie within a 20-minute drive of the killer's apartment. Only one banned guns, posting signs warning permit

holders that their guns weren't allowed. Yet, the killer didn't go to the theater that was closest to his home. Nor did he go to the largest theater. He went to the single one where he didn't believe that others would be able to protect themselves.[30]

Enforce Existing Laws

The United States already has sufficient gun control laws. The real problem is that they are not properly enforced. The government should enforce existing restrictions, not create unnecessary new ones. One example of lack of enforcement is the background check system. That system alerts law enforcement when a person who is not legally allowed to buy a gun tries to do so. However, the reality is that very few of these people are ever prosecuted. LaPierre insists that the background check system does not work, because no serious effort is made to actually enforce it. He says, "You had 76,000 prohibited people denied last year [2012], and only 13 were convicted by the federal government." He states, "I just don't believe this is a serious attempt to keep people safe. If it was a serious attempt to keep people safe, this administration would prosecute, under the existing federal gun laws, more than 13 out of the 76,000."[31] LaPierre and other critics argue that other gun control laws in the United States also receive lax enforcement. They insist that the answer to gun-related problems in the United States starts with enforcing existing laws.

Strictly enforcing existing laws also helps make it clear to society that gun-related violence is against the law and will be punished. Following the 2012 shooting at Sandy Hook Elementary School, many officials proposed new regulations, with the intent of preventing another shooting. However, Mark Mattioli, whose six-year-old son, James, died in the shooting, argues that such proposals are both unnecessary and useless. He insists that the real solution is to strictly enforce the many gun control laws that already exist. Mattioli says, "How do we expect to have any impact on a society and say, 'We're going to pass a law. Hey this is inexcusable. We can't allow any more of this. Let's pass a law that will change

Less Violent Crime in States with Right-to-Carry Gun Laws

Some people argue that allowing more people to carry guns actually deters crime because it means that citizens are not such easy targets for criminals. This graph supports such an argument by showing that over the past ten years, states that allow people to carry concealed handguns in public—right-to-carry (RTC) states— have lower violent crime rates than states that do not have right-to-carry gun laws. The chart compares the violent crime rate per 100,000 people for RTC and non-RTC states and shows that it is significantly lower in RTC states.

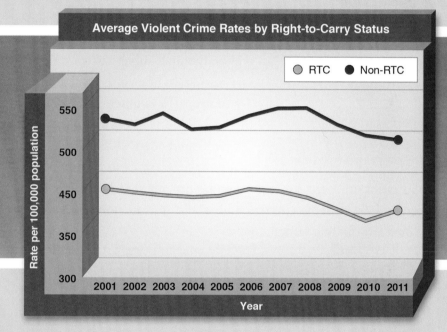

Source: Howard Nemerov, "State of the Second Amendment," PJ Media, February 14, 2013. http://pjmedia.com/blog.

the course of the future' when we don't enforce the laws that we have on the books—the most important laws?"[32]

No Universal Background Checks

Many gun control advocates argue that the United States should institute universal background checks in order to prevent criminals from obtaining guns; however, this will not only be ineffective but will infringe on

Americans' civil rights. Statistics do show that a significant number of gun transfers happen without a background check. It has been argued that if the government enforces universal background checks—where a background check occurs every time a gun is transferred between individuals—then it will be more difficult for criminals to obtain guns. However, the reality is that the law will have no impact on criminals, because they will still be able to obtain guns illegally. Law-abiding citizens with no criminal intent will be the ones subject to an unnecessary restriction of civil rights.

> "How do we expect to have any impact on a society and say, 'We're going to pass a law. Hey this is inexcusable. . .' when we don't enforce the laws that we have on the books—the most important laws?"[32]
>
> —Mark Mattioli, the father of six-year-old James, who died in the 2012 Sandy Hook Elementary School shooting.

Marion P. Hammer, past president of the NRA and executive director of Unified Sportsmen of Florida, argues that it makes no sense to require a background check in every situation. She points out that in many cases a background check is not needed and would impose unnecessary difficulty on a law-abiding citizen. She says:

> Imagine a grandfather who wants to give a family shotgun to his 12-year-old grandson having to do a background check on his grandson before giving him the shotgun. Or a friend having to do a background check on his lifetime best buddy before lending him a hunting rifle. Or, if your mother had a prowler at her home, having to do a background check on your own Mom before you could give her one of your guns for protection.[33]

NRA president David Keene agrees. He discusses proposed new gun restrictions such as universal background checks and says that they are the wrong solution to reducing gun violence. He says, "They interfere with people's rights without doing anything to solve the problem."[34]

Strict Laws Do Not Reduce Crime

Gun control advocates insist that more gun restrictions will make the United States safer; however, no evidence supports the idea that strict gun control and low rates of gun ownership will actually reduce violent crime in the United States. Senior editor of *Reason* magazine Brian Doherty argues that the data actually show the opposite. He says, "The constant expansion in gun ownership (with the number of new firearms entering American possession averaging around 4 million a year) and expanded rights to legally carry weapons have been accompanied by a 41 percent decline in violent crime rates over the past two decades."[35] Thomas Sowell, a fellow at the Hoover Institution, agrees that strict gun control laws do not reduce crime. He argues that such laws simply disarm law-abiding people, while criminals find a way to obtain guns no matter what the law is. He states that strong gun control laws are actually correlated with higher murder rates. For example, he says, "The rate of gun ownership is higher in rural areas than in urban areas, but the murder rate is higher in urban areas. The rate of gun ownership is higher among whites than blacks, but the murder rate is higher among blacks." According to Sowell, "For the country as a whole, hand-gun ownership doubled in the late 20th century, while the murder rate went down."[36]

Additional laws on who can purchase and carry guns will not make Americans safer and may actually reduce their safety. Instead of passing new laws, the United States should allow law-abiding citizens to own guns for self-defense and should prevent criminals from obtaining them by enforcing the laws that already exist.

Chapter Three

Should Certain Types of Guns and Ammunition Be Banned?

Certain Types of Guns and Ammunition Should Be Banned

- Assault weapons are inappropriate and dangerous for civilian use and should be banned.
- High-capacity ammunition clips result in more violent crime and should be banned.
- The former assault weapons ban helped reduce gun-related injury and death in the United States.
- The example of California proves that banning certain types of weapons and ammunition is beneficial.

The Debate at a Glance

Bans on Certain Types of Guns and Ammunition Are a Bad Idea

- Civilians need assault weapons and high-capacity ammunition clips for self-defense.
- Banning certain types of guns and ammunition would restrict the ability of Americans to enjoy shooting sports.
- The former assault weapon ban did not benefit the United States.
- Banning assault weapons and high-capacity ammunition clips will not eradicate them; it will simply encourage an illegal market for these items.

Certain Types of Guns and Ammunition Should Be Banned

"The ban on assault weapons and high-capacity ammunition magazines must be reinstated. Like assault weapons, high-capacity magazines are not used for hunting, do not belong in our homes and wreak havoc in our communities."

Jim Johnson, testimony at the Senate Judiciary Committee hearing, January 30, 2013. www.judiciary.senate.gov.

Consider these questions as you read:

1. How persuasive is the argument that assault weapons are meant for warfare and are inappropriate for civilian use? Explain.
2. Do you agree with the argument that high-capacity ammunition clips increase gun-related deaths and injury? Why or why not?
3. Some people believe the United States should institute another ban on assault weapons and high-capacity ammunition clips. Do you agree or disagree? Explain.

Editor's note: The discussion that follows presents common arguments made in support of this perspective, reinforced by facts, quotes, and examples taken from various sources.

Not all types of guns and ammunition are appropriate for widespread public ownership. Some should only be used by law enforcement or those in the military and should be banned for the general public. Assault weapons are one group of guns that should be banned. In the United States the term *assault weapon* is commonly used to refer to certain semiautomatic firearms with features similar to military firearms. (These guns are separate from true assault rifles, which are used only in the military.) A person with an assault weapon can quickly and easily harm or kill a large number of people. These weapons were designed for war, where the goal is to kill as many people as possible, and are not appropriate for widespread public ownership. Senator Dianne Feinstein, founder of a bill that would ban military-style assault weapons and high-capacity ammunition magazines, insists, "Weapons of war don't belong on our streets or in our theaters, shopping malls and, most of all, our schools."[37]

When these weapons of war are used in places such as schools and city streets, the results are devastating. For example, in the 2012 Sandy Hook Elementary School shooting, the shooter used an assault weapon with horrific results. In about ten minutes he was able to kill twenty-six people, shooting all of his victims multiple times. According to H. Wayne Carver, the chief state medical examiner, in the seven autopsies he personally conducted, there were three to eleven wounds apiece. He explains that the military-style assault rifle the shooter used is extremely harmful because the bullets do not just pass through the body, but explode throughout the tissue. Carver says, "I've been at this for a third of a century. . . . This probably is the worst I have seen or the worst that I know of any of my colleagues having seen."[38]

Inappropriate and Dangerous

Regular citizens have no need to own such powerful and dangerous weapons. While Americans may choose to own guns for hunting, target practice, or protection, they can satisfy these needs with less dangerous types of guns. Fourth-generation farmer John W. Boyd Jr. discusses his own use of guns and insists that assault weapons are completely unnecessary. He says that just like his father and grandfather, he owns a rifle for protection and hunting. He believes the Second Amendment guarantees that right; however, he also insists that the right is not without limits, and that one of those limits should be a ban on assault weapons. He says:

Like most farmers I have a deep appreciation for the land and the animals who share the land. I respect the right to bear arms and support the Second Amendment. But I question what the Sam Hill does a farmer or hunter need with an AR-15 or any assault weapon? What are you hunting that requires the need of a semi-automatic weapon—an instrument used for military warfare? This defies common sense.[39]

Ammunition

The United States should also ban high-capacity ammunition clips. Like assault weapons, high-ammunition clips are unnecessary for ordinary civilians to own, and they pose a threat to the safety of the general population because they allow a person to quickly fire many shots. Representative Mike Thompson says, "I've been a hunter all my life, and there's no reason to have a magazine that holds 30 shells. Call it what it is: an assault magazine. And we don't have any reason to assault anyone in our communities, in our neighborhoods. . . . Why do you need 30 shells in a magazine?"[40]

In a January 2013 statement about gun violence, the White House proposed that legislation be passed limiting ammunition magazines to ten rounds. It insists that high-capacity magazines contribute to many of the shooting deaths and injuries that occur in the United States. The White House says, "The case for prohibiting high-capacity magazines has been proven over and over; the shooters at Virginia Tech, Tucson, Aurora, Oak Creek, and Newton [mass shootings that occurred in the United States] all used magazines holding more than 10 rounds. . . . These magazines enable any semiautomatic weapon to be used as an instrument of mass violence."[41] An analysis of past mass shootings does suggest that casualties may have been lower if the shooters had not used high-capacity magazines. For example, in 2011 Jared Lee Loughner used a semiautomatic pistol with a thirty-three-round magazine to kill six people and wound twelve outside a grocery store in Tucson, Arizona. It was not until he stopped to reload that bystanders were able to tackle Loughner and

A Ban on High-Capacity Magazines Would Be Effective

The availability of high-capacity magazines in the United States means that criminals can more easily shoot and kill a greater number of people. Critics believe high-capacity magazines should be banned in order to reduce such gun-related death and injury. Research shows that the US ban on magazines with more than ten rounds (which was in place between 1994 and 2004 as part of the federal assault weapons ban) was effective because it reduced the use of high-capacity magazines. It reveals that this use decreased while the ban was in place and increased after the ban expired.

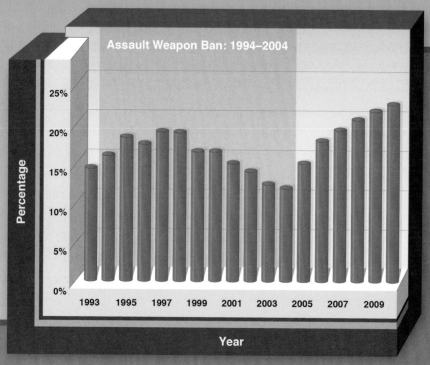

Share of guns recovered from crime scenes in Virginia that had high-capacity magazines

Assault Weapon Ban: 1994–2004

Source: Mayors Against Illegal Guns, "What We Stand For," 2013. www.demandaction.org.

stop him from shooting anyone else. If Loughner's gun had only held ten rounds instead of thirty-three, he may have inflicted much less injury before he was stopped. One of his victims, nine-year-old Christina Taylor Green, was killed with the thirteenth bullet in his gun, a bullet that would not have existed in a ten-round magazine.

Research shows that the availability of assault weapons and high-capacity magazines often results in more violent crime and a higher number of deaths. For example, the organization Mayors Against Illegal Guns analyzed fifty-six mass shootings that occurred in the United States between January 2009 and January 2013. It found that in the shootings where assault weapons or high-capacity magazines were used, an average of 135 percent more people were shot and 57 percent more deaths occurred than in other mass shootings.

Former Assault Weapon Ban

Between 1994 and 2004 the United States banned the manufacture and purchase of certain types of semiautomatic weapons and high-capacity magazines, and research indicates that this helped reduce gun-related injuries and deaths. For example, the *Washington Post* finds that the ban reduced the use of firearms with high-capacity magazines in crimes. Without high-capacity magazines, criminals are not able to inflict such a high number of injuries in such a short amount of time. Researchers for the *Post* study looked at data about the type of firearms that police in Virginia recovered from crime scenes. They found that in 1998—four years after the ban was instituted—the rate at which police recovered firearms with high-capacity magazines began to drop. It reached a low of 9 percent of the total number of guns recovered in 2004. In 2004 the ban expired, and the next year the rate of high-capacity magazines began to rise again, reaching 20 percent in 2010. Baltimore County police chief Jim Johnson agrees that the ban helped reduce gun-related violence. He believes

> "I have been in law enforcement for nearly 35 years, and have seen an explosion in firepower since the assault weapons ban expired."[42]
>
> —Jim Johnson, Baltimore County police chief.

the expiration of the ban has been associated with increasingly violent shootings. Says Johnson, "I have been in law enforcement for nearly 35 years, and have seen an explosion in firepower since the assault weapons ban expired. It is common to find many shell casings at crime scenes these days, as victims are being riddled with multiple gunshots."[42]

The only reason the former ban was not more effective is that it was not strict enough. It had too many exceptions and loopholes that still allowed people to obtain assault weapons and high-capacity magazines. For example, it only covered a limited number of guns. In addition, gun manufacturers could easily make small modifications to their weapons so that they no longer fell under the ban.

The California Example

The experience of California is an example of a strictly enforced ban on assault weapons and high-capacity magazines that has been extremely beneficial. The state prohibits the sale of numerous firearms that have been defined as assault weapons. It also prohibits the sale of magazines that hold more than ten rounds of ammunition. According to the *Los Angeles Times*, these rules have significantly reduced California's rate of firearms-related deaths. The *Times* reports that in 1981, before the current state gun laws were passed, the rate of firearms-related deaths in California was 16.5 per 100,000 people. By 2000 it had dropped to 9.18, and in 2010 it was only 7.9. The *Times* says, "The numbers strongly indicate that regulation works."[43] In fact, many people argue that the only reason California's laws do not work even better is that nearby states such as Arizona and Nevada do not also have strict laws, and Californians are able to purchase banned weapons there.

Certain types of guns and ammunition such as assault weapons and high-capacity magazines are responsible for a significant number of deaths and injuries in the United States and should be banned.

Bans on Certain Types of Guns and Ammunition Are a Bad Idea

"I don't believe that the banning of any class of weapon would solve the gun violence problem this country has."

Quoted in Matthew Cox, "Gun Makers: Assault Weapons Ban Will Kill Jobs," Military.com, January 18, 2013. www.military.com.

Critical Thinking Questions

1. Can you think of an example where a person might need a gun that can quickly fire multiple shots without being reloaded?

2. Many sports shooters argue that assault weapons and high-capacity magazines make the sport easier and more enjoyable. Do you think this is enough reason to prevent a ban on these types of weapons and ammunition? Explain your answer.

3. Taking into account the facts and arguments presented in this discussion, how persuasive is the argument that civilians need assault weapons and high-capacity ammunition clips? Which arguments provide the strongest support for this perspective, and why?

Editor's note: The discussion that follows presents common arguments made in support of this perspective, reinforced by facts, quotes, and examples taken from various sources.

Some people have proposed banning certain types of guns and ammunition in the United States, such as assault weapons and high-capacity magazines. (An assault rifle is a type of gun used in the military; however, in the United States the term *assault weapon* is often used to refer to certain semiautomatic firearms that have features similar to military firearms.) However, many people have a need for these types of weapons, and they should not be banned. One important use for assault weapons and high-capacity magazines is for self-defense. Former chief economist at the US Sentencing Commission John Lott argues that semiautomatic guns can save lives in cases when a person needs to defend him- or herself from an attacker. He points out, "Single shot rifles where you have to physically reload the gun may not do people a lot of good when they are facing multiple criminals or when their first shot misses or fails to stop an attacker."[44]

> "Single shot rifles where you have to physically reload the gun may not do people a lot of good when they are facing multiple criminals or when their first shot misses or fails to stop an attacker."[44]
>
> —John Lott, former chief economist at the US Sentencing Commission.

In 2010 a fifteen-year-old boy in Houston, Texas, used an AR-15—often called an assault weapon—to defend himself and his younger sister after two men broke into their home. After he shot them, the invaders fled and were arrested when they showed up at the hospital. The website Guns Save Lives argues that the boy may not have been as successful at defending himself if he had a different type of gun. It says, "It should be pointed out that due to the ease of use, good accuracy and light recoil of the AR15 platform that even a 15 year old boy was able to successfully wield it with precision and great accuracy."[45]

The ability to own certain types of semiautomatic guns is particularly important for women who want to have the ability to defend themselves. Gayle Trotter, a lawyer and senior fellow at the Independent Women's Forum, argues that some assault weapons, like the AR-15, are particularly good for women's self-defense because they are easy to hold and use and also because they look intimidating. She explains, "The peace of mind that a woman has as she's facing three, four, five violent attackers, intruders in her home, with her children screaming in the background—the peace of mind that she has knowing that she has a scary-looking gun gives her more courage when she's fighting hardened, violent criminals." Trotter says that banning assault weapons will disproportionately harm women. She explains, "If we ban these types of assault weapons, you are putting women at a great disadvantage, more so than men, because

Assault Weapons Are Not the Cause of Most Gun-Related Deaths

A ban on assault weapons is not an effective way to address the problem of gun-related deaths in the United States because the majority of deaths are not caused by these types of guns. While there are varying definitions of what an assault weapon is, the majority of firearms that people refer to as "assault weapons" are actually rifles. This chart shows the types of firearms used in homicides in the United States in recent years, as reported by the FBI. It reveals that the vast majority of firearm-related homicides between 2007 and 2011 involved handguns. Rifles, on the other hand, were used much less frequently in firearm-related killings.

Murder Victims, by Weapon 2007–2011					
Weapon	2007	2008	2009	2010	2011
Total firearms	10,129	9,528	9,199	8,874	8,583
Handguns	7,398	6,800	6,501	6,115	6,220
Rifles	453	380	351	367	323
Shotguns	457	442	423	366	356
Other guns	116	81	96	93	97
Firearms, type not stated	1,705	1,825	1,828	1,933	1,587

Source: Federal Bureau of Investigation, "Murder Victims by Weapon, 2007–2011," *Crime in the United States, 2011.* www.fbi.gov.

they do not have the same type of physical strength and opportunity to defend themselves in a hand-to-hand struggle. And they're not criminals; they're moms. They're young women. And they're not used to violent confrontations."[46]

Target Practice

The types of semiautomatic guns and high-capacity magazines that gun control advocates want to ban are also important for target shooting, a popular sport in the United States. Taking away these weapons would greatly restrict the freedom of Americans to enjoy sports shooting. For example, gun owner Delma Blinson discusses high-capacity magazines, insisting that a sport shooter needs them for numerous reasons. First, he says, high-capacity magazines are cheaper and easier to carry around than lower-capacity ones. In addition, he says, using a high-capacity magazine saves time on reloading. He believes this is important at the shooting range. He says, "It is a rather tedious task, especially for older people with stiff joints. If you are using a popular range and most of the stations are being used you don't want to be rude to anyone waiting their turn by taking time to load rounds into your magazines while you occupy a shooting station. It's a courtesy thing."[47]

Unfounded Fears

The belief that certain types of guns and ammunition are a threat to Americans and need to be banned is based on fear and not supported by facts. Simply calling certain types of guns "assault weapons" exaggerates their danger. Tim Macy, vice chair of the national gun lobby Gun Owners of America, says, "So-called 'assault weapons' are not designed to assault anyone—they are 'defense weapons' for Americans to defend our families, our country and our Constitution."[48] Many people insist that assault weapons are similar to those used by the military and thus dangerous for civilian use. However, this is also untrue. Macy maintains that these semi-automatic guns are nothing like the real assault weapons used by the military. In fact, he says, "They are functionally not different than many pistols or shotguns which have been available to civilian markets for over a century."[49] Calling them assault weapons is misleading and makes them seem dangerous, when they are actually no more dangerous than other commonly used types of guns, such as pistols.

> "So-called 'assault weapons' are not designed to assault anyone—they are 'defense weapons' for Americans to defend our families, our country and our Constitution."[48]
>
> —Tim Macy, vice chair of the national gun lobby Gun Owners of America.

Former Ban Accomplished Nothing

Between 1994 and 2004 the United States did ban certain types of guns and ammunition, and the ban did not significantly reduce gun-related violence. Under the ban, certain types of semiautomatic weapons—known as assault weapons—and magazines with more than ten rounds were prohibited. However, research shows that banning these weapons was not effective at reducing crime. The National Institute of Justice commissioned the University of Pennsylvania to study the ban, and the researchers found that while gun violence was reduced over the time that the ban was in place, this was unrelated to the ban. They state: "We cannot clearly credit the ban with any of the nation's recent drop in gun violence. And, indeed, there has been no discernible reduction in the lethality and injuriousness of gun violence."[50]

One reason that the former ban was ineffective—and any future one would be, too—is that these types of weapons are generally only used in a small number of crimes. For example, assault weapons are not the guns responsible for most gun-related violence. So banning them is not an effective way to reduce that violence. The University of Pennsylvania researchers report that the formerly banned assault weapons were only used in about 2 to 8 percent of gun crimes. Thus, banning them is unlikely to make people much safer. The *Economist* says, "The great bulk of America's murders are committed with 'ordinary' handguns, not the sort that would be covered by any remotely likely ban."[51] In 2011 approximately eighty-five hundred people died from firearms in the United States. However, most of these deaths—about sixty-two hundred—were from handguns, not assault rifles.

Even in mass shootings, assault weapons are not the most common type of gun used. In an analysis of mass shootings since 1982, *Mother Jones* finds that of the 143 total guns used by the shooters, only 20 were assault weapons. Mayors Against Illegal Guns conducted its own analysis, finding that of fifty-six mass shootings between January 2009 and January 2013, assault weapons or high-capacity magazines were used in only 23 percent of the incidents.

Impossible to Eradicate

Banning a certain type of weapon or ammunition will not eradicate them from use in the United States; it will simply create an underground market for them. Anyone who wants to obtain such items will be able to do so, but instead of purchasing them legally, they will do so illegally. J.D. Tuccille, the managing editor of *Reason 24/7*, describes how easy it was for him to purchase a gun illegally. He says that New York's restrictive gun laws made it very difficult for him to legally purchase a pistol. The restrictions, however, did not stop him from ultimately obtaining a gun; they simply pushed him into doing it on the black market instead. According to Tuccille, this was actually far easier than the legal process and relatively inexpensive. He says, "It took an email, a phone call, and a friendly meeting, and for less than 300 bucks, I was the proud owner of a semi-automatic variant of an AK-47—the famed assault rifle of the old Soviet bloc and of guerrilla fighters everywhere." He says, "As it turned out, the illicit rifle was not only cheaper and easier to obtain than the legal pistol, but the seller was much more pleasant to deal with than the cops administering the official process."[52]

The United States should not ban certain types of guns and ammunition. Doing so would restrict Americans' freedom to protect themselves and to enjoy shooting sports. In addition, it would do little to prevent gun-related violence.

Chapter Four

Can Stronger Gun Control Measures Prevent Mass Shootings?

Stronger Gun Control Measures Will Prevent Mass Shootings

- Stronger gun control measures will prevent shootings by making it more difficult for shooters to obtain guns.
- While it is unlikely that stronger gun control will eliminate shootings, it will be effective because it will reduce shootings and the harm they cause to society.
- Mass shootings have been significantly reduced in other countries following the adoption of stronger gun control measures.
- While some people argue that people need guns to protect themselves from shooters, research shows that armed civilians rarely prevent shootings.

The Debate at a Glance

Stronger Gun Control Measures Will Not Prevent Mass Shootings

- A person intent on committing a mass shooting will be able to obtain a gun no matter what the laws are.
- Stronger gun control laws will mean that victims are unarmed and unable to protect themselves from shooters.
- Allowing people to carry guns actually deters mass shooters, so the government should not strengthen gun control laws.
- Mental illness is the real cause of many mass shootings, so the government should address that instead of focusing on stronger gun control.

Stronger Gun Control Measures Will Prevent Mass Shootings

"The more you tighten the law, the more you reduce the risk [of another mass shooting.]"

Quoted in Rowena Mason, "Connecticut School Shooting: Gun Controls Reduce Risk of Massacres, Says Jack Straw," *Telegraph* (London), December 16, 2012. www.telegraph.co.uk.

Consider these questions as you read:

1. Mass shooter Radcliffe Haughton was able to easily obtain a gun online, and the next day he used it to shoot his wife and several other people. Do you think stronger gun control measures would have stopped Haughton from obtaining the gun? Why or why not?

2. Do you agree with the argument that stronger gun control will be effective even if it does not completely eliminate mass shootings? Explain.

3. Australia has almost eliminated mass shootings since it instituted stronger gun control measures. Do you think such measures would be effective in the United States? Why or why not?

Editor's note: The discussion that follows presents common arguments made in support of this perspective, reinforced by facts, quotes, and examples taken from various sources.

In October 2012, three days after his wife obtained a restraining order against him for domestic violence, Wisconsin resident Radcliffe Haughton placed a want ad on ArmsList.com, one of the largest online gun sites in the United States. According to news reports, the ad read: "Looking to buy ASAP. Prefer full size, any caliber. Email ASAP. I constantly check my emails. Hoping it has a high mag capacity with the handgun, ammo, accessories. I am a serious buyer. Email me ASAP. Have cash now and looking to buy now. I am mobile." Haughton was legally prohibited from purchasing a gun because of the restraining order, and the urgency of his posting suggested he might intend to use the gun for harm. However, through the website, he was easily and quickly able to purchase a gun from a private seller. Gun and security expert Pablo Valasquez insists that a responsible gun seller would not have sold a gun to the person who made this posting. He says, "There are several red flags here. Stay away from this. You don't want to sell to this person. There's a high urgency to have this firearm. The fact that he'll take any firearm and he's not looking for a particular firearm to add to his collection simply states 'I need a firearm and I need it now.' All these things are red flags not to sell to this person."[53] The next day Haughton went to the spa where his wife worked and used that gun to kill three people, including his wife. He injured four others and then killed himself.

Making It More Difficult to Obtain Guns

Stronger gun control measures will help prevent shootings like this by making it more difficult for potential shooters to obtain weapons. Under current regulations, it is relatively easy for anyone to obtain a gun, regardless of their criminal record or any signs that they may use the gun for harm, as Haughton did. Research shows that many mass shooters obtain their guns legally. For example, in a 2012 investigative report published in *Mother Jones*, the author analyzes sixty-two mass shootings from the past thirty years and reports that almost 80 percent of the killers got their weapons legally. Tougher gun control could make it more difficult for potential shooters to obtain weapons.

Harm Reduction

Critics argue that stronger gun control is pointless because a potential shooter will find a way to get a gun, regardless of the law. Such criticism misses the point of gun control, which is intended to reduce shootings even if it is impossible to eliminate them. Society has many laws intended to prevent crime—for example, murder is illegal—and it does not give up on enforcing these laws just because they are not 100 percent effective. Law professor Jay Sterling Silver points out:

> No one would argue, for example, that homicide laws have no place on the books just because a legal proscription can't prevent all killings. . . . The fact that a law won't completely eradicate a particular harm is not an argument against its adoption. This holds true for gun regulation. The point is that, as with *all* law designed to protect life and limb, tighter gun control laws will reduce the carnage.[54]

Canadian journalist Emma Teitel compares the United States with Canada, which already has stronger gun control measures. She argues that Canada's laws might not eliminate shootings, but they definitely reduce the harm that these shootings cause. She says:

> There's been a spate of public shootings in the recent past where I live, for instance—an extraordinary number by Canadian standards—but the one source of comfort for me is the fact that the people responsible . . . were not carrying assault weapons like James Holmes was in Colorado [in 2012]. The main reason is that such weapons are illegal for private citizens to own in this country. Have the shootings here been tragic? Undeniably. Could they have been worse? Undeniably. The law did not work perfectly, but it worked somewhat. And that somewhat, for the people who avoided being killed in the shootings here, was a blessing.[55]

Evidence from Other Nations

Evidence from other countries reveals that stronger gun control measures do help reduce mass shootings. Jonathan Masters, a writer for the Council on Foreign Relations, compares global gun policies and finds that "democracies that have experienced similar traumatic shooting incidents [to those in the United States], for instance, have taken significant steps to regulate gun ownership and restrict assault weapons. They generally experience far fewer incidents of gun violence than the United States."[56] One example of this is Australia. In 1996 a gunman opened fire on tourists at a Tasmanian resort, killing thirty-five and wounding twenty-three—the worst mass shooting in Australia's history.

> "The point is that, as with *all* law designed to protect life and limb, tighter gun control laws will reduce the carnage."[54]
>
> —Jay Sterling Silver, a law professor.

In response, the government instituted strict new gun laws, including banning assault weapons, prohibiting private sales, and requiring gun registration. It also spent millions of dollars buying existing guns from private owners. There has been only one mass shooting since then. Says journalist Larry Womack, "In the 18 years prior to 1996 gun control reforms, that nation saw 13 mass shootings. In the 16 since, they have seen one—which usually isn't even counted, because the shooter was only able to kill two people before he had to stop to reload. . . . After that incident, Australia reviewed and tightened its gun laws again. Ten years later, there hasn't been another."[57]

Reducing Casualties

Even if stricter gun control does not eliminate mass shootings, it is likely to make them less deadly. Stricter laws would mean that would-be shooters are less likely to have as many weapons or such deadly weapons, meaning that they may inflict less damage. For example, Aurora, Colorado, shooter James Holmes used a semiautomatic gun to kill twelve people and injure fifty-eight. It is widely argued that Holmes was very intelligent and would have found a way to obtain weapons even in the face of stricter laws. However, author and political columnist Joe Klein argues that a ban on assault weapons might

Mass Shooters Have Easy Access to Guns

It is far too easy for a potential mass shooter to obtain a gun in the United States. Weak gun laws mean that even if an individual has a criminal record or mental health problems, he or she can purchase a gun, often without a background check. Of the mass shootings that occurred between 1982 and 2012, the majority of shooters obtained their weapons legally. To prevent mass shootings, the United States needs stronger gun control measures that will reduce such easy access to guns.

Mass Shootings in United States, 1982–2012

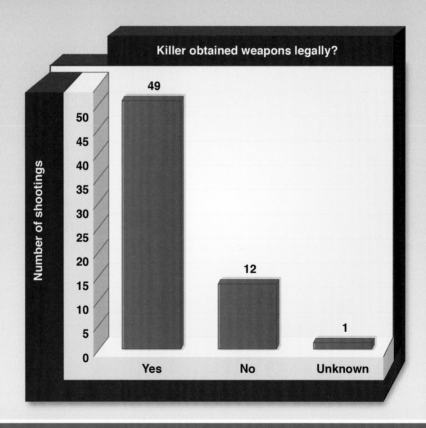

Killer obtained weapons legally?

Source: Mark Follman, Gavin Aronsen, and Deanna Pan, "A Guide to Mass Shootings in America," *Mother Jones*, February 27, 2013. www.motherjones.com.

have reduced the severity of the shooting. He says, "If the shooter had gone into the theater without a semiautomatic weapon, how many fewer would have been wounded? If only one person had escaped injury the law would be worth it."[58]

In China, a country with extremely strict gun laws, a 2012 incident shows that even though it may be impossible to prevent people from trying to harm others, gun control can effectively reduce casualties. On the same day that Adam Lanza killed twenty children in Connecticut, thirty-six-year-old Min Yongjun went on a rampage in a central China school with a knife. He injured twenty-three children, leaving some with severed ears and fingers and one with a fractured skull. However, the *Economist* points out, "Every country has its madmen, but Min was armed only with a knife, so none of his victims died."[59]

Armed Civilians Rarely Prevent Shootings

Some people insist that stronger gun control will simply disarm law-abiding citizens, making it more difficult for them to fight back against shooters. However, research shows that in most mass shootings, having armed civilians did nothing to help the victims. In a 2012 investigative report published in *Mother Jones*, the authors analyzed sixty-two mass shootings from the past thirty years and found that "in not a single case was the killing stopped by a civilian using a gun." In fact, says the report, "in recent rampages in which armed civilians attempted to intervene, they not only failed to stop the shooter but also were gravely wounded or killed."[60]

> "We need to do more to keep guns out of the wrong hands in the first place."[61]
>
> —Sandra J. Wortham, whose brother, Thomas, was shot dead outside their parents' home in Chicago in 2010.

Sandra J. Wortham's story supports this argument. Her brother, Thomas, was shot dead outside their parents' home in Chicago by robbers in 2010, even though he and his father, a retired police sergeant, fired back. Wortham says, "The fact that my brother and father were armed that night did not prevent my brother from being killed." In her opinion fewer guns, not more, is the answer. She says, "We need to do more to keep guns out of the wrong hands in the first place."[61]

It is far too easy for a person intent on carrying out a mass shooting to obtain a gun or even multiple guns. Stronger gun control will make it more difficult and help prevent mass shootings in the future.

Stronger Gun Control Measures Will Not Prevent Mass Shootings

"Mass killers are unwavering in their determination to carry out their mission; there is little that we can do to prevent them."

James Alan Fox, "Column: President's Plan Won't Stop Mass Killings," *USA Today*, January 16, 2013. www.usatoday.com.

Consider these questions as you read:

1. Do you agree with the argument that if an individual is determined to carry out a mass shooting, it is impossible to stop him or her? Why or why not?

2. Some people argue that the best way to prevent mass shootings is to allow more people to be armed so that mass shooters cannot so easily shoot whomever they choose. Do you agree with this perspective? Explain.

3. Taking into account the facts and arguments presented in this discussion, how persuasive is the argument that stronger gun control measures will not prevent mass shootings? Which arguments provide the strongest support for this perspective?

Editor's note: The discussion that follows presents common arguments made in support of this perspective, reinforced by facts, quotes, and examples taken from various sources.

Norway has some of the strictest gun control laws in the world. Anyone who wants to buy a gun must provide a valid reason for ownership and obtain a license from the government. Strict laws also govern gun storage, and police have the right to inspect an owner's home to ensure that they are following these laws. Yet despite such regulations, in 2011 Norwegian Anders Behring Breivik was able to carry out one of the deadliest mass shootings in history. After setting off a bomb in the capital city of Oslo, he took multiple guns to a summer camp at a nearby island, where he used them to kill sixty-nine people and injure more than one hundred. Breivik later revealed that he had been planning the attack for years. In his fifteen-hundred-page manifesto, which reveals his plans for the attack, he talks about how easy it was to conceal his true intentions while obtaining a gun in Norway. He says, "On the application form I stated: 'hunting deer'. It would have been tempting to just write the truth; 'executing category A and B cultural Marxists/multiculturalist traitors' just to see their reaction."[62]

Impossible to Stop

As this incident reveals, people intent on committing a mass shooting can do so even if they live in a place like Norway, where gun control laws are extremely strict. This means that stronger gun control measures are not the way to prevent mass shootings. James Alan Fox, author of *Extreme Killing: Understanding Serial and Mass Murder*, argues that mass shooters will find a way to kill people no matter what the law is. He says:

> Tighter restrictions . . . may help reduce America's gun violence problem generally, but mass murder is unlike most other forms of violent conflict. Mass killers are determined, deliberate and dead-set on murder. They plan methodically to execute their victims, finding the means no matter what laws or other impediments the state attempts to place in their way. To them, the will to kill cannot be denied.[63]

Politician Mitt Romney agrees. He discusses the 2012 Aurora, Colorado, shooting, in which a shooter entered a movie theater with multiple firearms, killing twelve people and injuring fifty-eight. Romney points out, "A lot of what this young man did was clearly against the law. But the fact that it was against the law did not prevent it from happening."[64]

Citizens Unable to Defend Themselves

Not only do stronger gun control laws fail to prevent mass shootings, they may actually harm society by disarming citizens, leaving them defenseless and an easy target for a shooter. Analysis of past shootings shows that most of them occur in places where people are prohibited from carrying guns, such as schools, and victims and bystanders are thus unarmed and unable to take action to stop the shooter. Former chief economist at the US Sentencing Commission John Lott says, "With just one single exception, every public shooting since at least 1950 in the United States in which three or more people have been killed has taken place where citizens are not allowed to carry guns." He argues that this is because many shooters intentionally go to places where they know people will not be able to defend themselves. Lott says, "If a violent criminal were ever stalking you or your family, would you put a sign in front of your home announcing that you didn't own a gun? Probably not. Yet, even though no one puts up those signs in front of their homes, we put up those signs on all sorts of other areas."[65] Critics argue that the effect of strong gun control laws may actually be to increase the chances of a shooting.

> "Tighter restrictions . . . may help reduce America's gun violence problem generally, but mass murder is unlike most other forms of violent conflict."[63]
>
> —James Alan Fox, author of *Extreme Killing: Understanding Serial and Mass Murder.*

Based on her own experience, Suzanna Gratia Hupp argues that people need to be allowed to carry guns in order to protect themselves from shootings. In 1991 she was in a cafeteria in Killeen, Texas, when a gunman smashed his truck through the front of the restaurant and fatally shot twenty-three people, including her parents. Hupp had left her own gun in her car because under Texas law she was not allowed to bring it into the restaurant. She argues that she should have been allowed to carry her gun in order to protect herself. She says, "I can't begin to get across to you how incredibly frustrating it is to sit there, like a fish in a barrel,

No Relationship Between Gun Control and Mass Shootings

Some people believe that stronger gun control measures will prevent mass shootings. However, the data reveals that shootings and the number of people injured or killed by them fluctuate randomly and unpredictably, unrelated to laws. This graph charts these fluctuations, showing that even in the years that the assault weapons ban was in effect (1994–2004) a significant number of people were killed and injured in mass shootings.

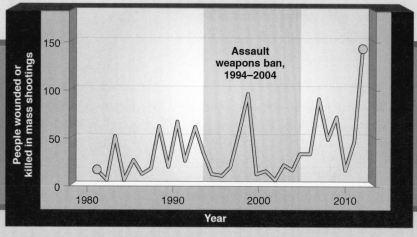

Source: Brad Plumer, "Everything You Need to Know About the Assault Weapons Ban, in One Post," *Washington Post*, December 17, 2012. www.washingtonpost.com.

and wait for it to be your turn, with no hope of defending yourself." She added, "The only thing the gun laws did that day was prevent good people from protecting themselves."[66] After the shooting, Hupp became a strong advocate of the individual right to carry a concealed weapon.

Guns Are a Deterrent

The best way to prevent future mass shootings is not to pass more gun control laws, but to increase the number of people who own and carry guns in order to protect the population and deter future shooters. Wayne LaPierre, CEO of the NRA, insists that no matter what the law is, there are certain to be future mass shooters. He says, "Our society is populated by an unknown number of genuine monsters—people so deranged, so evil, so possessed by voices and driven by demons that no sane person can possibly *ever* comprehend them. . . . Does anybody really believe that the next Adam Lanza isn't planning his attack on a school he's identified *at this very moment?*"[67] LaPierre argues that people need guns to protect themselves from such monsters. He maintains that if Sandy Hook Elementary School had had an armed security guard, twenty-six children may not have died that day.

Mental Illness Is the Problem

A significant number of mass shootings are carried out by people who are mentally ill. Thus, one of the most effective ways to prevent future shootings is to focus on identifying and treating mental illness, not trying to change gun control laws. In a 2012 report *Mother Jones* analyzed the mass shootings that have happened in the United States since 1982 and found that the majority of the shooters were mentally ill and that many showed signs of it before they carried out the shooting.

For example, in 2011 Jared Lee Loughner killed thirteen people in a mass shooting after showing signs of mental illness. Investigators later found that prior to the shooting, Loughner had shown signs of mental illness. *Time* magazine reports, "In his community-college classes, he would laugh randomly and loudly at nonevents. He would clench his fists and regularly pose strange, nonsensical questions to teachers and fellow students. 'A lot of people didn't feel safe around him,' [said] a former classmate."[68] Prior to the shooting, Loughner was expelled from Pima Community College and advised not to return until he had clearance from a mental health professional. Yet following his expulsion, Loughner was still able to pass a federal background check and purchase a handgun at a sporting goods store.

> "Federal and state funding of critical mental health services is under siege. Across the country, states facing severe financial shortfalls have reduced public mental health funding."[69]
>
> —The APA, an organization that represents psychiatrists in the United States.

63

Loughner's case and others like it reveal that the United States needs to take action to better recognize and treat mental illness to help prevent mass shootings. According to the American Psychiatric Association (APA), a mentally ill person is much less likely to commit a violent act if he or she is engaged in appropriate mental treatment. However, says the APA, America's mental health system does not currently receive enough funding to help all the people it should:

Federal and state funding of critical mental health services is under siege. Across the country, states facing severe financial shortfalls have reduced public mental health funding by $4.35 billion from 2009 to 2012. . . . Twenty-nine states have reported that fiscal and other pressures have caused them to close more than 3,200 psychiatric inpatient beds in the past four years. . . . Unfortunately, the promise of better access to psychiatric treatment will not be a reality absent requisite federal and state funding. In the wake of the Newtown tragedy, we hope that Congress will act to protect federal funding for mental health and addiction treatment research and services.[69]

Mass shootings are a problem in the United States. According to an analysis of these events since 1982 by *Mother Jones*, 2012 was the deadliest year, with almost eighty killed in mass shootings. The United States should try to prevent mass shootings from occurring; however, instituting stronger gun control is not the solution.

Source Notes

Overview: Gun Control and Violence

1. Joe Klein, "How the Gun Won," *Time*, August 6, 2012. www.time.com.
2. Mark Follman, "More Guns, More Mass Shootings—Coincidence?," *Mother Jones*, September 26, 2012. www.motherjones.com.
3. Christopher Matthews, "3 Approaches to Curbing Gun Violence—Using Economics," *Time*, December 18, 2012. www.time.com.

Chapter One: Do Americans Have a Constitutional Right to Own Guns?

4. Second Amendment Foundation, "SAF Gun Rights Frequently Asked Questions." www.saf.org.
5. Quoted in Jack Brammer, "Kentucky Sheriff Says He Won't Enforce New Gun Laws He Considers Unconstitutional," Kentucky.com, January 14, 2013. www.kentucky.com.
6. Quoted in Phil Gast, "Oklahoma Mom Calling 911 Asks If Shooting an Intruder Is Allowed," CNN, January 4, 2012. www.cnn.com.
7. Jack Kenny, "Gun Control or Killer Control? After Shooting Incidents in Which Multiple Victims Are Killed, Calls Arise for Gun Control. But Evidence Tells Us That Guns Control Wanton Killers, and Without Guns, Deaths Rise," *New American*, October 8, 2012. www.thenewamerican.com.
8. Kenny, "Gun Control or Killer Control?"
9. Barack Obama, speech at the National Urban League Convention, New Orleans, July 25, 2012.
10. Mark Udall, "What I'm Working On: Hunting, Fishing, and 2nd Amendment Rights," Mark Udall: US Senator for Colorado. www.markudall.senate.gov.
11. US Supreme Court, *District of Columbia v. Heller*, 2008. No. 07-290.
12. US Supreme Court, *McDonald v. Chicago*, 2010. No. 08-1521.

13. Linton Weeks, "The Second Amendment: 27 Words, Endless Interpretations," *NPR*, January 9, 2013. www.npr.org.

14. Keith Darling-Brekhus, "The Original Intent of the 2nd Amendment Was Not to Facilitate Citizen Rebellion," *Examiner*, January 21, 2013. www.examiner.com.

15. Quoted in Azmat Khan, "How Conservatives 'Reinvented' the Second Amendment," *Frontline*, December 18, 2012. www.pbs.org.

16. Quoted in Khan, "How Conservatives 'Reinvented' the Second Amendment."

17. Debra Maggart, "Even Friends Must Toe the Line or Face Wrath," *New York Times*, December 17, 2012. www.nytimes.com.

18. *Democracy in America* (blog), *Economist*, "Gun Rights: A Stinger for Antonin," July 30, 2012. www.economist.com.

19. Erika Christakis, "The Myth of Second Amendment Exceptionalism," *Time*, December 18, 2012. www.time.com.

20. US Supreme Court, *District of Columbia v. Heller*.

Chapter Two: Are More Restrictions on Who Can Purchase and Carry Guns Needed?

21. Quoted in City of New York, "Gun Show Undercover: Arizona," January 2011. www.gunshowundercover.org.

22. Obama, speech at the National Urban League Convention.

23. Quoted in Jeffrey Goldberg, "The Case for More Guns (and More Gun Control)," *Atlantic*, December 2012. www.theatlantic.com.

24. Quoted in Eileen Sullivan, "Gun Control Efforts Complicated by Maze of U.S. Gun Laws," *Huffington Post*, January 25, 2013. www .huffingtonpost.com.

25. Jeff McMahan, "Why 'Gun Control' Is Not Enough," *New York Times*, December 19, 2012. www.nytimes.com.

26. Larry Womack, "If Gun Control Doesn't Work, Why Does Congress Need Metal Detectors?," *Huffington Post*, December 19, 2012. www .huffingtonpost.com.

27. Fareed Zakaria, "The Solution to Gun Violence Is Clear," *Washington Post*, December 19, 2012. www.washingtonpost.com.

28. Wayne LaPierre, NRA Press Conference, National Rifle Association, December 21, 2012. http://home.nra.org.

29. Quoted in Goldberg, "The Case for More Guns."

30. John Lott, "Gun Restrictions Leave People Vulnerable and Helpless," *U.S. News & World Report*, December 19, 2012. www.usnews.com.

31. Quoted in Anthony Licata, "The F&S Gun Rights Interviews: Wayne LaPierre, Executive Vice President and CEO, National Rifle Association," *Field & Stream*, February 28, 2013. www.fieldandstream.com.

32. Quoted in Billy Hallowell, "'The Problem Is Not Gun Laws': Watch the Emotional Speech by a Sandy Hook Victim's Dad That Got a Standing Ovation," TheBlaze, January 28, 2013. www.theblaze.com.

33. Marion P. Hammer, "'Universal Background Checks'—Absolutely Not," AmmoLand, January 23, 2013. www.ammoland.com.

34. Quoted in Candy Crowley, "State of the Union with Candy Crowley," CNN, January 13, 2013. www.cnn.com.

35. Brian Doherty, "Gun Control Couldn't Have Stopped It: The Tucson Massacre Should Not Lead to New Restrictions on Firearms," *Reason*, April 2011. www.reason.com.

36. Thomas Sowell, "Gun-Control Ignorance," *National Review*, December 18, 2012. www.nationalreview.com.

Chapter Three: Should Certain Types of Guns and Ammunition Be Banned?

37. Dianne Feinstein, "Feinstein Statement on Connecticut School Shooting," December 14, 2012. www.feinstein.senate.gov.

38. Quoted in Susan Candiotti and Dana Ford, "Connecticut School Victims Were Shot Multiple Times," CNN, December 15, 2012. www.cnn.com.

39. John W. Boyd Jr., "A Farmer's Perspective on Guns and the Second Amendment," *Huffington Post*, January 17, 2013. www.huffington post.com.

40. Quoted in Bill Briggs, "Gun Control Advocates Zero In on New Tactic: Banning High-Capacity Ammo Clips," NBC News, January 7, 2013. www.nbcnews.com.

41. White House, "Now Is the Time: The President's Plan to Protect Our Children and Our Communities by Reducing Gun Violence," January 16, 2013. www.whitehouse.gov.

42. Jim Johnson, testimony at the Senate Judiciary Committee hearing, January 30, 2013. www.judiciary.senate.gov.

43. Michael Hiltzik, "Taking Aim at the Gun Industry," *Los Angeles Times*, February 16, 2013. www.latimes.com.

44. Lott, "Gun Restrictions Leave People Vulnerable and Helpless."

45. Guns Save Lives, "Son Uses Dad's AR-15 to Defend Home (2010)," July 4, 2010. www.gunssavelives.net.

46. Quoted in *Wall Street Journal*, "'Scary Looking' Guns and Women's Self Defense," January 30, 2013. www.wsj.com.

47. Delma Blinson, "What Liberals Need to Understand About 'Gun Guys/Gals,'" *Beaufort Observer* (Beaufort County, NC), March 9, 2013. www.beaufortobserver.net.

48. Tim Macy, "Let's Change the Terminology in Defending Our Gun Rights," Gun Owners of America, January 8, 2013. www.gunowners.org.

49. Macy, "Let's Change the Terminology in Defending Our Gun Rights."

50. Christopher S. Koper, Daniel J. Woods, and Jeffrey A. Roth, "An Updated Assessment of the Federal Assault Weapons Ban: Impacts on Gun Markets and Gun Violence, 1994–2003," Report to the National Institute of Justice, US Department of Justice, June 2004. www.sas.upenn.edu.

51. *Economist*, "Newtown's Horror; Gun Violence in America," December 22, 2012. www.economist.com.

52. J.D. Tuccille, "Gun Restrictions Have Always Bred Defiance, Black Markets," *Reason*, December 22, 2012. http://reason.com.

Chapter Four: Can Stronger Gun Control Measures Prevent Mass Shootings?

53. Quoted in Myra Sanchick, "Gun and Security Expert Says He Would Not Have Sold to Radcliffe Haughton," Fox6Now.com, October 25, 2012. http://fox6now.com.

54. Jay Sterling Silver, "Will Gun Control Reduce, Stop Mass Murder? NRA Says 'No', Presents Alternative," Alaska Dispatch, December 21, 2012. www.alaskadispatch.com.

55. Emma Teitel, "The Arms Race No One Is Talking About," *Maclean's*, August 2, 2012. www2.macleans.ca.

56. Jonathan Masters, "U.S. Gun Policy: Global Comparisons," Council on Foreign Relations, December 21, 2012. www.cfr.org.

57. Womack, "If Gun Control Doesn't Work, Why Does Congress Need Metal Detectors?"

58. Klein, "How the Gun Won."

59. *Economist*, "Newtown's Horror."

60. Follman, "More Guns, More Mass Shootings."

61. Quoted in Associated Press, "Sen. Cruz: Constitutional Gun Rights Must Be Protected 'Not Just When Popular,'" CBS Local, February 12, 2013. http://washington.cbslocal.com.

62. Quoted in *Telegraph* (London), "Norway Shooting: Quotes from Anders Behring Breivik's Online Manifesto," August 19, 2011. www.telegraph.co.uk.

63. James Alan Fox, "Gun Control or Carry Permits Won't Stop Mass Murder," CNN, July 21, 2012. www.cnn.com.

64. Quoted in Garrett Haake, "Romney on NBC: Changing Gun Laws Won't 'Make All Bad Things Go Away,'" NBC News, July 25, 2012. www.nbcnews.com.

65. Lott, "Gun Restrictions Leave People Vulnerable and Helpless."

66. Quoted in Associated Press, "Sen. Cruz."

67. LaPierre, NRA Press Conference.

68. Kate Pickert and John Cloud, "If You Think Someone Is Mentally Ill: Loughner's Six Warning Signs," *Time*, January 11, 2011. www.time.com.

69. American Psychiatric Association, statement at Mental Health Services Working Group public hearing testimony, Connecticut General Assembly, December 20, 2012. www.cga.ct.gov.

Gun Control and Violence Facts

Gun Laws

- According to a December 2012 Gallup poll in which 1,038 adult Americans were surveyed, 58 percent of respondents were in favor of strengthening laws that cover the sale of firearms.
- In a December 2012 poll of 620 adults, CNN found that 53 percent of respondents believed that shootings will continue to happen, regardless of government or societal actions to prevent such shootings.
- In 2010 the National Instant Criminal Background Check System ran nearly 16.5 million background checks for firearms purchases. Only 0.48 percent of these purchases were denied.
- The Violence Prevention Research Program at the University of California–Davis estimates that identifying prohibited persons through background checks and denying their firearm acquisitions reduces the risk of their committing new firearm-related or violent crimes by approximately 25 percent.

Gun-Related Violence

- The United Nations Office on Drugs and Crime reports that firearms were responsible for 10,300 homicides in the United States in 2009, compared with 8,804 in Mexico and 12,808 in Colombia.
- According to a 2012 report by *Mother Jones*, since 1982 at least sixty-two mass shootings in thirty states occurred in the United States.
- A 2010 Centers for Disease Control and Prevention report found that firearms were responsible for 19,392 suicides in the United States.
- The Brady Campaign to Prevent Gun Violence reports that every day in the United States, a total of approximately eight children and

teens die from gun violence, and thirty-eight are shot but survive their injuries.

- According to data from the Federal Bureau of Investigation, more than two-thirds of the homicides that occurred in the United States in 2011 involved a firearm.

Gun Ownership

- According to the Small Arms Survey, the estimated total number of guns held by US civilians is 270 million—88.9 firearms per 100 people. India ranks second, with an estimated 46 million guns in private hands—or about 4 firearms for every 100 people.
- In a 2011 survey of 1,005 adult Americans, Gallup found that 47 percent have a gun in their home or somewhere on their property.
- The Small Arms Survey reports that of twenty-eight countries it surveyed for a 2011 report on firearms, only the United States and Yemen consider gun ownership to be a basic right.
- In a 2012 report, the Congressional Research Service found that the most recent estimate of the number of guns in the United States is about 310 million (in 2009).

Assault Weapons and High-Capacity Magazines

- The organization Mayors Against Illegal Guns analyzed fifty-six mass shootings that occurred between January 2009 and January 2013. It found that at least thirteen involved assault weapons or high-capacity magazines.
- In a December 2012 Gallup poll in which 1,038 adult Americans were surveyed, 44 percent of respondents were in favor of a ban on semiautomatic guns, also known as assault rifles.
- In a 2012 analysis of mass shootings in the United States, *Mother Jones* magazine found that of the sixty-two such shootings carried out since 1982, half of the shooters used high-capacity magazines, with more than ten rounds.

Gun Sales

- The Bureau of Alcohol, Tobacco, Firearms and Explosives reports that in 2010, nearly 5.5 million new firearms were manufactured in the United States, nearly all (95 percent) for the US market. An additional 3.25 million firearms were imported into the United States.
- According to Mayors Against Illegal Guns, a national survey of inmates shows that nearly 80 percent of those who used a handgun in a crime acquired it in a private transfer.
- According to the Bureau of Alcohol, Tobacco, Firearms and Explosives, more than 129,817 federally licensed firearms dealers exist in the United States.
- The organization Mayors Against Illegal Guns reports that in December 2012 more than twenty thousand guns were for sale on ArmsList.com, and more than 85 percent of the listings were placed by private sellers.

Related Organizations and Websites

Brady Campaign to Prevent Gun Violence
1225 Eye St. NW, Suite 1100
Washington, DC 20005
phone: (202) 898-0792 • fax: (202) 371-9615
website: www.bradynetwork.org

The Brady Campaign works to enact and enforce regulations and public policies that will increase public awareness and reduce gun violence in the United States. Its website provides facts, studies, reports, and information on current and proposed legislation—all in connection with guns in the United States.

Coalition to Stop Gun Violence (CSGV)
1424 L St. NW, Suite 2-1
Washington, DC 20005
phone: (202) 408-0061
e-mail: csgv@csgv.org • website: www.csgv.org

The CSGV seeks to reduce gun violence through research and effective policy advocacy. Its members include religious organizations, child welfare advocates, public health professionals, and social justice organizations. Its website has information about various issues related to gun control.

Gun Owners of America (GOA)
8001 Forbes Pl., Suite 102
Springfield, VA 22151
phone: (703) 321-8585 • fax: (703) 321-8408
website: www.gunowners.org

The GOA is a nonprofit lobbying organization formed in 1975 to preserve and defend the Second Amendment rights of gun owners. It believes firearms ownership is an important freedom of Americans and represents gun owners when their rights are threatened.

Law Center to Prevent Gun Violence
268 Bush St. #555
San Francisco, CA 94104
phone: (415) 433-2062 • fax: (415) 433-3357
website: http://smartgunlaws.org

The Law Center to Prevent Gun Violence is a nonprofit organization that is dedicated to preventing deaths caused by guns. Its website provides information about America's gun control laws.

Mayors Against Illegal Guns
website: www.mayorsagainstillegalguns.org

Mayors Against Illegal Guns is a coalition of more than 850 mayors from cities across the country. It works to share information and develop policies and laws that will help law enforcement target illegal guns. Its website has information about gun laws and illegal use of guns in the United States, as well as reports and editorials about illegal guns.

National Rifle Association of America (NRA)
11250 Waples Mill Rd.
Fairfax, VA 22030
phone: (800) 672-3888
website: www.nra.org

Founded in 1871, the NRA believes that Americans have a constitutional right to own firearms. It promotes gun safety through training and education.

Second Amendment Foundation
12500 NE Tenth Pl.
Bellevue, WA 98005
phone: (425) 454-7012 • fax: (425) 451-3959
website: www.saf.org

The Second Amendment Foundation believes Americans have a constitutional right to own firearms. It argues that this right should be granted to all citizens, except violent criminals. The organization works to inform the public about the consequences of gun control.

Violence Policy Center (VPC)
1730 Rhode Island Ave. NW, Suite 1014
Washington, DC 20036
phone: (202) 822-8200
website: www.vpc.org

The VPC is a nonprofit organization that works to stop gun-related death and injury through research, advocacy, education, and collaboration. It believes that firearms should be subject to health and safety regulations, just like other consumer products are. Its website has information about firearms laws and numerous reports about gun-related violence and death.

For Further Research

Books

Matt Doeden, *Gun Control: Preventing Violence or Crushing Constitutional Rights?* Minneapolis, MN: Twenty-First Century, 2012.

Brian Kevin, *Gun Rights & Responsibilities*. Minneapolis, MN: Abdo, 2012.

Robert Spitzer, *The Politics of Gun Control*. Boulder, CO: Paradigm, 2012.

Glenn Utter, *Encyclopedia of Gun Control and Gun Rights*. Amenia, NY: Grey House, 2011.

Craig Whitney, *Living with Guns: A Liberal's Case for the Second Amendment*. New York: Public Affairs, 2012.

Periodicals

Max Fisher, "A Land Without Guns: How Japan Has Virtually Eliminated Shooting Deaths," *Atlantic*, July 2012.

Jeffrey Goldberg, "The Case for More Guns (and More Gun Control): How Do We Reduce Gun Crime and Aurora-Style Mass Shootings When Americans Already Own Nearly 300 Million Guns?," *Atlantic*, December 2012.

Jill Lepore, "Battleground America," *New Yorker*, April 23, 2012.

Fareed Zakaria, "The Solution to Gun Violence Is Clear," *Washington Post*, December 19, 2012.

Internet Sources

City of New York, "Gun Show Undercover: Arizona," January 2011. www.gunshowundercover.org/report.

Mark Follman, Gavin Aronson, and Deanna Pan, "A Guide to Mass Shootings in America," *Mother Jones*, December 15, 2012. www.mother jones.com/politics/2012/07/mass-shootings-map.

Jonathan Masters, "U.S. Gun Policy: Global Comparisons," Council on Foreign Relations, December 21, 2012. www.cfr.org/united-states /us-gun-policy-global-comparisons/p29735?cid=nlc-public-the_world _this_week-link4-20121221?cid=otr-partner_site-pbs_newshour.

Mayors Against Illegal Guns, "Analysis of Recent Mass Shootings," 2013. http://libcloud.s3.amazonaws.com/9/56/4/1242/analysis-of-recent -mass-shootings.pdf.

Lydia Saad, "Americans Want Stricter Gun Laws, Still Oppose Bans," Gallup, December 27, 2012. www.gallup.com/poll/159569/americans -stricter-gun-laws-oppose-bans.aspx.

White House, "Now Is the Time: The President's Plan to Protect Our Children and Our Communities by Reducing Gun Violence," January 16, 2013. www.whitehouse.gov/sites/default/files/docs/wh_now_is_the _time_full.pdf.

Index